Salahddine Krit

Towards Excellence:

Salahddine Krit

Towards Excellence:

Ibnou Zohr University Development Plan 2024-2028

ScienciaScripts

Imprint

Any brand names and product names mentioned in this book are subject to trademark, brand or patent protection and are trademarks or registered trademarks of their respective holders. The use of brand names, product names, common names, trade names, product descriptions etc. even without a particular marking in this work is in no way to be construed to mean that such names may be regarded as unrestricted in respect of trademark and brand protection legislation and could thus be used by anyone.

Cover image: www.ingimage.com

This book is a translation from the original published under ISBN 978-620-7-47962-7.

Publisher:
Sciencia Scripts
is a trademark of
Dodo Books Indian Ocean Ltd. and OmniScriptum S.R.L publishing group

120 High Road, East Finchley, London, N2 9ED, United Kingdom
Str. Armeneasca 28/1, office 1, Chisinau MD-2012, Republic of Moldova, Europe
Printed at: see last page
ISBN: 978-620-8-25045-4

Contents

PREAMBLE

The development of the Moroccan university is a priority in national policy, in order to play its role as a place of knowledge and culture, and to meet the needs of the economic and industrial market as a source of skills, the elite and the citizens of tomorrow.

The major challenge facing Moroccan universities is to provide the country's various socio-economic sectors with the skills they need to implement the government's "major projects policy", embodied in sectoral development plans, programs, projects and strategies: Pacte national pour l'émergence industrielle et nouveaux métiers mondiaux du Maroc (Offshoring, automotive, aeronautics and space, electronics, textiles and leather, agri-food); Plan AZUR, Plan Maroc Vert ... These skills needs require more students to be oriented towards scientific, technical and vocational branches.

In line with such a proactive policy, Moroccan universities need to be integrated into the socio-economic development process to meet the challenge of market needs in terms of human resources and provide the skills required for quality-training and innovation-research.

Major projects are currently underway to guarantee this development approach. To this end, His Majesty King Mohamed VI has clearly expressed his desire to make our country an attractive and competitive investment platform.

It is in this favorable context, whether on a national, international or regional level, that I propose a development plan for Ibnou Zohr Agadir University in line with :

- ❖ The Royal Vision of the Educational System;
- ❖ The National Initiative for Human Development INDH ;
- ❖ Orientations of the National Charter for Education and Training ;
- ❖ Framework Law on Higher Education (Law 01-00)
- ❖ the Strategic Vision of the 2015-2030 Reform launched by the Conseil Supérieur de l'Education, de la Formation et de Recherche Scientifiques ;
- ❖ The Department's Action Plan 2017-2022;
- ❖ Framework law 51-17 on the reform of the education, training and scientific research system;
- ❖ Ibn Zohr University Development Project;
- ❖ National Plan to Accelerate the Transformation of the ESRI Ecosystem (PACTE ESRI 2030)

In accordance with the law on the organization of higher education (law no. 01-00), the position of Dean and Director in the Moroccan university has evolved considerably. While the responsibilities have remained the same, in terms of ensuring the smooth running of the institution and its integration within the university and with society, the way in which they are exercised and the conditions under which they are carried out have been greatly transformed. The position of Director still implies the capacity for vision, conviction and a strong sense of leadership, but it now requires that this vision and leadership be exercised in a context of openness to both internal and external partnerships, e.g. the Director's external presence to raise the profile of the establishment, seek funding, obtain collaborations and negotiate agreements, etc. It requires teamwork, sensitivity to the community and its aspirations, and the ability to read and share the issues at stake with the grassroots, using simple management tools that promote fast, transparent and efficient operations. In a context of competition and limited resources, it also implies collective choices. It's a tough but extraordinary human challenge.

This development project for the Ibnou Zohr Agadir University sets out the vision, strategy and approach for making this university a place of quality education, a center for research and innovation, and a tool for socio-economic development at both regional and national levels.

This project is submitted in response to the call for candidates for the position of President of Université Ibnou Zohr Agadir. It follows on from a very long experience at the Université Ibnou Zohr, first as a teacher-researcher since 2010 and Filière coordinator 2011-2015 and Director of a Research Laboratory 2018-2022, then as Head of the Mathematics, Computer Science and Management Department of the Faculté Polydisciplinaire de Ouarzazate since 2015-2020, and then as President and organizer of several International Conferences since 2016, and finally as Head of the Computer Science Department of this establishment since 2022.

My various teaching, research and professional activities, as well as all the administrative responsibilities I have exercised throughout my academic and industrial career, have enabled me to develop a thorough understanding of the workings of the national university system, to appropriate the concepts and principles of higher education reform and to tackle the many aspects of its implementation.

My candidacy for the position of President of UIZ Agadir is also motivated by my determination to continue contributing to the cultural, scientific and technical development of Université Ibnou Zohr, in all five regions.

It is for all these reasons that I submit this project for the development of UIZ Agadir, while hoping to have the opportunity to accomplish this task with efficiency and relevance.

The development project for the period 2024-2028 is framed by the Royal Guidelines cited in the following extracts from the speeches of His Majesty King Mohammed VI:

SA MAJESTÉ LE ROI MOHAMMED VI
QUE DIEU L' ASSISTE

Extracts from speeches by His Majesty King Mohammed VI o n National Education, Higher Education, Scientific Research and Innovation

"...The judicious reform of the education and training system is the essential path to take if we are to meet the challenges of development, because it must be recognized that this is not a simple sectoral reform, but a salutary struggle in the face of a huge challenge. To achieve this, we have no choice but to promote research and innovation, and to upgrade our human resources, which are our main asset...".

(Extract from the speech by His Majesty the King on Throne Day, July 30, 2009).

"...We also expect this governance to contribute to strengthening the foundations of national solidarity and consolidating social justice, which is founded on the pursuit of the education system's recovery process.
This requires a heightened awareness of the importance of the progress made in this area, and a better grasp of the long road still ahead.
It is therefore necessary to deploy constant and sustained efforts, and to be firmly convinced of the crucial role of the national school system as a privileged space for the expression of the principle of equality of opportunity and initiation to the virtues of citizenship, and as an inexhaustible resource at the service of human development...".

(Extract from the speech by His Majesty the King at the opening of the 1st Session of the 3rd legislative year, October 09, 2009).

"...In my opening speech to Parliament, I stressed the need to place youth issues at the heart of the new development model. I also called for an integrated strategy dedicated to young people, which would define the means to effectively promote their status.
Indeed, a young person cannot be called upon to play his role and fulfill his duty without first having benefited from the necessary opportunities and qualifications...".

"... Indeed, we must no longer accept that our education system functions as a machine for producing legions of unemployed people, especially in certain university courses whose graduates, as everyone knows, struggle enormously to enter the job market..."

"...Moreover, when a large number of young people, especially those with advanced degrees in scientific and technical fields, think of emigrating, they are not only motivated by the tempting incentives of life abroad. They are also considering this possibility because in their own country they lack a climate and conditions conducive to active life, professional advancement, innovation and scientific research...".

" ... We therefore call on the government and other stakeholders to take, as soon as possible, a series of measures aimed in particular at achieving the following objectives

"... - First: undertake a comprehensive overhaul of public support mechanisms and programs for youth employment, to make them more effective and tailored to young people's expectations. This overhaul must follow the model I advocated in the Speech from the Throne, with regard to social protection programs..."

"... - Secondly: give priority to specialties that are employable, and set up an effective early guidance system in the second or third year before the baccalauréat. Its role is to help students, according to their aptitudes and inclinations, to make one or other of two choices: to embark on a university course or vocational training..."

"... - Thirdly: thoroughly review vocational training specialties so that they meet the needs of companies and the public sector, and are in step with the transformations underway in the industrial and professional sectors. In this way, graduates will have a better chance of integrating professionally..."

"... - Fourth: Put in place practical mechanisms to qualitatively improve incentives for young people to set up small and medium-sized businesses in their specialist fields, and to support self-employment and social enterprise initiatives..."

"... - Fifth: introduce new mechanisms for integrating part of the informal sector into the formal sector, by providing the human potential of the informal sector with appropriate training, incentives and social coverage, and by supporting their self-employment or business creation projects...".

"... - Sixth: set up a compulsory three- to six-month program at each school to bring students and trainees up to speed in foreign languages; promote greater linguistic integration at all levels of study, particularly in the teaching of scientific and technical subjects...
" **(Extract from the speech of His Majesty the King on the occasion of the 65thanniversary of the Revolution of the King and the People, August 20, 2018).**

VISION

Higher education systems have always focused on knowledge and scientific research, playing a key role in the creation, preservation and transmission of these resources for the benefit of the community. Over the last few decades, these systems have undergone significant transformations to better meet the needs of contemporary society. These changes have mainly focused on improving competitiveness in training to meet market needs, on innovation-oriented scientific research, and on improving the quality of services offered to students and businesses.

Since the promulgation of Law 01.00, major efforts have been made to improve Moroccan higher education and adapt it to the country's ambitions. These initiatives include the implementation of the LMD (Licence, Master, Doctorat) system and the 2009-2012 Emergency Program, which established a contractual relationship between the State and universities, with monitoring of university projects based on precise objectives and quantifiable indicators. This program was designed to meet specific expectations, such as improving intake capacity, raising graduation rates, boosting scientific output and improving university governance.

However, despite the financial support provided to the Moroccan university within this framework, certain structuring objectives have not been fully achieved, particularly with regard to :

- The effectiveness of organizational bodies ;
- Professionalization, diversification and relevance of university offerings;
- Diversification and rationalization of financial resources ;
- Involvement in more active university teaching innovation;
- The development of targeted research and R&D in partnership with the regional socio-economic fabric;
- Extending and sustaining ongoing staff training.

The royal speech of August 20, 2013 was a decisive moment for collective awareness of the state of the education system in Morocco. H.M. King Mohammed VI drew a harsh and forthright conclusion on the situation of public education and training in the country, describing it as worrying. The speech, which was truly striking, warned those involved in education and called for a general mobilization to rectify a situation deemed alarming.

1. **Structural and organizational shortcomings:** The speech revealed the many flaws that weaken the Moroccan education system. These include ineffective management of resources, dysfunction within the responsible bodies, and an organization unable to meet the growing needs of the student population.
2. **Quality of education:** The quality of education was strongly criticized, with the discourse emphasizing that the public system was failing to meet expectations in both vocational training and general education. Pupils and students were often ill-prepared to face the demands of the modern job market.
3. **Unequal access to education:** His Majesty the King also highlighted the marked disparities in access to education between the different regions of the country, and between public and private education. These inequalities are a major obstacle to equal opportunities, an essential foundation for Morocco's social and economic development.
4. **School dropout and unemployment:** The phenomenon of school dropout and the high unemployment rate among young graduates have been identified as critical issues. These issues reflect the inability of the education system to ensure effective professional integration for young Moroccans.
5. **Call for rapid, far-reaching reform:** In response to this alarming situation, the King called for urgent, coherent reform, insisting on the rapid adoption of the texts relating to the Higher Council for Education, Training and Scientific Research, as provided for in the Constitution. This council was seen as a crucial element in guiding and structuring the reform of the education sector.
6. **Mobilizing players:** The royal speech was also a call to collective action, calling for the mobilization of all players in the education sector, including the government, teachers, parents and economic partners. It was not just a question of recognizing the challenges, but also of actively engaging in a process of transforming the education system.

Since that speech, several initiatives have been undertaken to address these challenges, such as the implementation of the 2015-2030 Strategic Vision and the enactment of Framework Law 51-17. Despite these efforts, challenges remain, and the success of these reforms will depend on political will and the ability of stakeholders to maintain a lasting commitment.

These efforts took shape with the formalization of contracts between the supervisory ministry and the universities, marked by the signing of the 2021-2023 program contracts.

Université Ibnou Zohr Agadir is now committed to adopting new strategies for teaching, research and innovation, and to strengthening more effective and proactive governance. These strategies have become a necessity, dictated by the regulatory framework of Framework Law 51-17 and the national context of regionalization, as described in the Regional Performance Framework (2015-2030), which aims to "preserve achievements, strengthen weaknesses, and meet expectations". This framework enables the university to seize the opportunities offered by the five regions.

In these regions, public higher education is represented by all the establishments of Ibnou Zohr University, aiming to create an attractive dynamic by integrating research, training and engineering in conjunction with companies and local authorities in the regions.

Université Ibnou Zohr Agadir, which occupies an important place in the Moroccan university landscape thanks to its positioning in the country's economic capital, has unique opportunities at its disposal. These environmental assets must be exploited to continue to assert its role as an institution for the production and dissemination of knowledge, as well as a key player in the regional value chain and a lever for the development of each region's intangible capital.

The Ibnou Zohr Agadir University development project for the period 2024-2028 is a continuation of previous government efforts. The project aims to reinforce actions already implemented, while exploring new avenues to accelerate the university's development. The aim is to enable the university to adapt its strategies and consolidate its position as a key player in the Moroccan educational landscape, by proactively responding to society's emerging needs and fostering rapid, sustained evolution.

The Ibnou Zohr Agadir University development project aims to continue the government's efforts, building on existing initiatives and exploring new avenues to accelerate its development. It aims to actively involve all stakeholders in the implementation of Framework Law 51-17, and to capitalize on existing achievements. The aim is to transform the university into :

- An institution that offers, in all its establishments, a unique student experience, based on quality training and innovative research activities, fostering an interdisciplinary scientific culture rooted in national and global challenges;
- An open and plural university, attentive to the needs and concerns of its region and society, helping to create an environment conducive to the respect, fulfillment, commitment and well-being of its community;
- A university renowned for its efficient organizational model, combining a collegial, participatory approach with simple, effective administrative and decision-making processes;
- A humanist university, committed to promoting the arts and training a new generation aware of the major issues facing society at regional, national and international levels.

I. <u>University context</u>

I.1 Ibnou Zohr University

UIZ is governed by law no. 01-00 on the organization of higher education, and has legal personality and administrative and financial autonomy. Its mission is to contribute to the development of research, the dissemination of knowledge and culture, the preparation of young people for the world of work, notably through the development of know-how, and regional and national growth.

The university provides :
- Initial and continuing training;
- Scientific and technological research ;
- Carrying out expert appraisals ;
- Contribution to the country's overall development ;
- International cooperation.

1. History and foundations

Created in 1989 (the Faculty of Arts and Humanities and the Faculty of Science had existed since 1984, when they were part of Cadi Ayyad University in Marrakech). Unique in its region, it is a major player and driving force in the development of higher education and research in Morocco's southern and Saharan provinces. Its main vocation is to encourage and strengthen research as a means of creating and renewing knowledge, with the aim of promoting the blossoming of students' intellectual, moral and cultural capacities in all fields of knowledge, so that they can demonstrate scientific, technological and artistic creativity, as well as critical thinking.

2. Number of students

- **Total student enrolment**: Approximately 150,000 students, divided into different educational cycles (bachelor's, master's, doctorate).
- **Proportion of girls**: Around 50% of total enrolment, illustrating the strong participation of women in higher education.

3. Teachers and Staff

- **Number of teaching staff** : More than 1,600 teaching and research staff across all disciplines.

- **Administrative and technical staff**: Around 1,000 people, contributing to the smooth running of the university.

4. Training offer

- **Number of degree courses**: Over 150 degree courses, covering a wide range of fields including science, arts, humanities, law, economics, engineering and information technology.
- **Number of master's programs**: Approximately 100 master's programs, focusing on research and advanced specialization.
- **Doctoral programs**: The university offers several doctoral schools with hundreds of doctoral students enrolled in various research fields.
- **Continuing education**: The university also offers continuing education programs for professionals wishing to improve their skills.

5. Scientific research

- **Research laboratories**: Over 100 laboratories and research centers, covering fields such as life sciences, exact sciences, humanities and social sciences.
- **Scientific publications**: Hundreds of articles published every year in national and international journals, reflecting our intense research activity.
- **International partnerships**: The university collaborates with a number of institutions around the world, taking part in joint research projects and academic exchange programs.

6. Infrastructure

- **Campuses**: The university has several modern campuses equipped with libraries, laboratories, sports facilities and student residences.
- **Libraries**: Several university libraries, with thousands of books, journals and digital resources available to students and researchers.
- **Sports facilities**: The university is equipped with sports fields, gymnasiums and other facilities to promote sports and extracurricular activities.

7. Success rates and employability

- **Success rate**: The success rate for final exams varies from course to course, with an average of 70% for bachelor's and master's courses.

- **Graduate employability**: A majority of the university's graduates find employment within two years of graduation, particularly in engineering, economics and management sciences.

8. Economic and social impact

- **Regional contribution**: Ibnou Zohr University plays a crucial role in the socio-economic development of the Souss-Massa region and beyond, by training skilled executives and supporting innovation and applied research.
- **Community involvement**: The university is actively involved in local development projects, including education, health and sustainable development initiatives.

Ibnou Zohr University is a pillar of higher education in southern Morocco, with a significant influence on regional development. Its figures illustrate not only its importance as an academic institution, but also its key role in innovation, research and the training of future generations.

The Ibnou Zohr University of Agadir covers five regions:

- The Souss-Massa region,
- The Guelmim-Oued Noun region,
- The Laâyoune-Saguia al Hamra region,
- Dakhla-Oued Ed-Dahab region
- The Drâa-Tafilalet region.

II. <u>Regional context</u>

II.1 Regional Economic Analysis: Dynamics and Potential of Morocco's Southern Regions

❖ Geographical position and climate

- **Geographical position**: These regions are located in the south of Morocco, encompassing desert, coastal and mountainous areas. Their strategic position between the Atlantic and the Sahara makes them important crossroads for economic exchanges, particularly with sub-Saharan African countries.
- **Climate**: The climate is predominantly arid to semi-arid, with low and irregular rainfall, which has a strong influence on economic activities, particularly agriculture and livestock farming.

❖ Infrastructure and Accessibility

- **Infrastructure**: Over the past few decades, these regions have benefited from considerable investment in infrastructure. The construction of roads, airports, ports and other public infrastructure has facilitated the integration of these regions into the national and international economy.
- **Accessibility**: Coastal regions such as Souss-Massa, Laâyoune-Saguia al Hamra and Dakhla-Oued Ed-Dahab have ports that connect them directly to international markets. Other regions, although less accessible, benefit from improved road networks.

❖ Economic potential and key sectors

- **Agriculture and fisheries**: These regions are home to some of the country's most productive agricultural areas (such as Souss-Massa) as well as significant fisheries resources, particularly along the Atlantic coast.
- **Tourism**: The potential for tourism is considerable, with unique landscapes such as the Sahara dunes, oases and beaches. Saharan and coastal tourism are booming, attracting investment in tourism infrastructure.
- **Renewable energies**: Strong sunshine and coastal winds offer enormous potential for the development of renewable energies, particularly solar and wind power, with several projects underway or in the planning phase.

❖ Socio-economic challenges

- **Regional equity**: Despite economic progress, there are significant disparities in terms of development between urban and rural areas, as well as between the regions themselves. Some areas remain marginalized, with limited access to basic services.

- **Unemployment and Migration**: Unemployment, particularly among young people, remains a major challenge. This drives many residents to migrate to the big cities or seek opportunities abroad.
- **Natural resource management**: Water scarcity, desertification and the sustainable management of natural resources are crucial to the long-term development of these regions.

❖ Regional and International Cooperation

- **Cooperation**: These regions, especially those close to borders, play a strategic role in Morocco's relations with neighboring countries, particularly in terms of trade and security cooperation.
- **Foreign investment**: The creation of free zones and tax incentives is attracting foreign investment, particularly in the tourism, fishing and renewable energies sectors.

The regional context of Morocco's southern regions is characterized by a combination of high economic potential and socio-economic challenges. These regions play a crucial role in Morocco's development strategy, particularly in terms of integrating less developed regions into the national economy and enhancing the country's competitiveness on the international stage.

1. Souss-Massa region

- **Regional capital**: Agadir
- **Population**: approx. 2.7 million
- **Economy** :
  - **Agriculture**: The region is one of Morocco's leading agricultural areas, renowned for its citrus fruit, fruit and vegetable production. The agricultural sector employs a significant proportion of the population.
  - **Tourism**: Agadir is a major tourist destination with a well-developed hotel infrastructure. Tourism plays a key role in the local economy.
  - **Industry**: The region has a diversified industrial base, including food processing, building materials and textiles.
  - **Fishing**: Agadir is also an important center for the fishing industry, with one of the country's largest fishing ports.

2. Guelmim-Oued Noun region

- **Regional capital** : Guelmim
- **Population**: Approximately 500,000
- **Economy** :
  - **Livestock farming**: Livestock farming is a predominant economic activity, particularly camel farming.
  - **Agriculture**: The region has considerable agricultural potential, particularly in the oases, where dates and other drought-resistant crops are grown.
  - **Tourism**: Saharan tourism, with attractions such as sand dunes and cultural festivals, contributes to the region's economic development.
  - **Handicrafts**: Handicrafts, especially the production of traditional carpets and jewelry, play an important role in the local economy.

3. Laâyoune-Saguia al Hamra region

- **Regional capital**: Laâyoune
- **Population**: Approximately 500,000
- **Economy** :
  - **Fishing**: The region has vast fishery resources, notably through the port of Laâyoune, which is a major center for the fishing industry.

- **Extractive industry**: The region's phosphate deposits make mineral extraction a significant part of the economy.
- **Renewable energies**: The region has great potential in renewable energies, particularly wind and solar power.
- **Infrastructure**: The region has seen significant investment in infrastructure, with the construction of roads, ports and other public facilities to support economic development.

4. Dakhla-Oued Ed-Dahab region

- **Regional capital**: Dakhla
- **Population**: Approximately 200,000
- **Economy** :
  - **Fishing**: Fishing is the region's most developed economic sector, with ports exporting fish products to Europe and other markets.
  - **Tourism**: Tourism, particularly niche tourism such as kitesurfing and ecotourism, is developing rapidly in the region.
  - **Agriculture**: Farming, particularly livestock breeding and greenhouse cultivation, is expanding with the use of modern irrigation techniques.
  - **Free trade zones**: The Dakhla region is home to a number of free trade zones, which attract foreign investment, particularly in seafood processing.

5. Drâa-Tafilalet region

- **Regional capital** : Errachidia
- **Population**: approx. 1.6 million
- **Economy** :
  - **Tourism**: The region is famous for its desert landscapes, kasbahs and historic sites, attracting many tourists.
  - **Agriculture**: Agriculture in the oases, with the cultivation of dates, cereals and fruit, plays a central role in the economy.
  - **Handicrafts**: Handicrafts, particularly the production of pottery and traditional textiles, are an important source of income for the local population.
  - **Energy**: The region has potential in renewable energies, notably through solar power plant projects.

Conclusion

Morocco's five regions boast an economic diversity marked by a combination of traditional sectors such as agriculture, fishing and crafts, and new sectors such as tourism and renewable energies. Each region has its own economic specificities and makes its own unique contribution to the country's overall development.

III. <u>Ibnou Zohr University in figures and data</u>

➢ Supervision :

- **1592 Teachers;**
- **634 Administrative and technical staff ;**
  For 147806 registered students, i.e. average student-teacher ratios (2023-2024) :
- **Educational = 1/93**
- **Administrative =1/233**

By 2024-2025, the number of students is expected to exceed 150,000, with over 500 doctoral students.

➢ Training courses :

The training catalog includes :
- **100** Licences Fondamentales **(LF)**, **17** Licences Professionnelles **(LP), 14** Licence d'excellence **(LE)**;
- **05** Bachelor of Education **(LE)** ;
- **61** Masters and **10** specialized Masters;
- **21** University Technology Diplomas (**DUT**);
- **11** Engineering diplomas (DI);
- **12** ENCG diploma ;
- **03** Courses for the Diplôme de Docteur en Médecine (DM);
- **03** Doctoral study centers (CED);

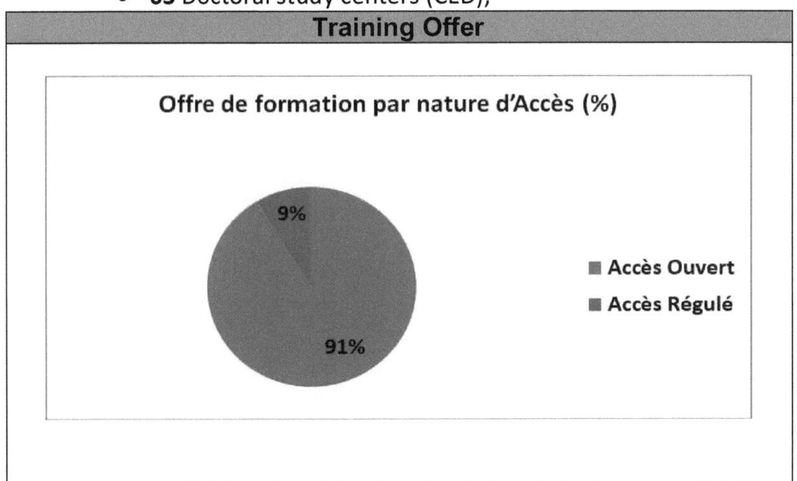

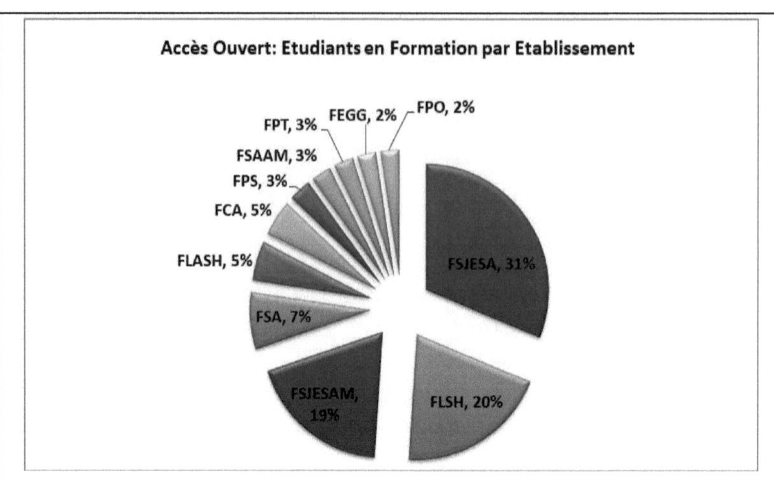

Accès Ouvert: Etudiants en Formation par Etablissement
FPT, 3%
FEGG, 2%
FPO, 2%
FSAAM, 3%
FPS, 3%
FCA, 5%
FLASH, 5%
FSA, 7%
FSJESA, 31%
FSJESAM, 19%
FLSH, 20%

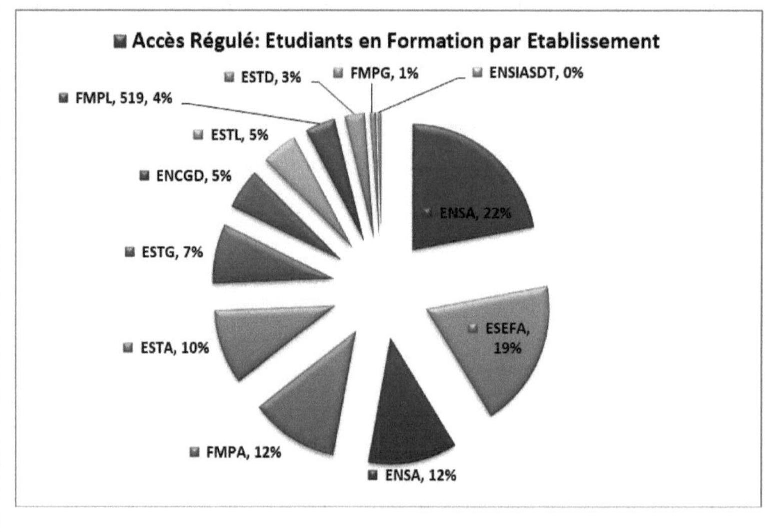

Accès Régulé: Etudiants en Formation par Etablissement
ESTD, 3%
FMPG, 1%
ENSIASDT, 0%
FMPL, 519, 4%
ESTL, 5%
ENCGD, 5%
ENSA, 22%
ESTG, 7%
ESTA, 10%
ESEFA, 19%
FMPA, 12%
ENSA, 12%

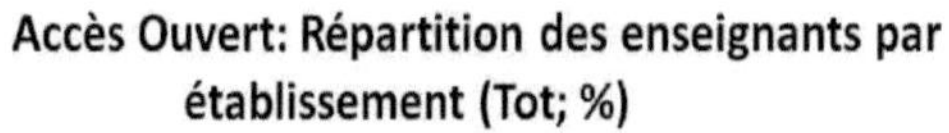

Accès Ouvert: Répartition des enseignants par établissement (Tot; %)

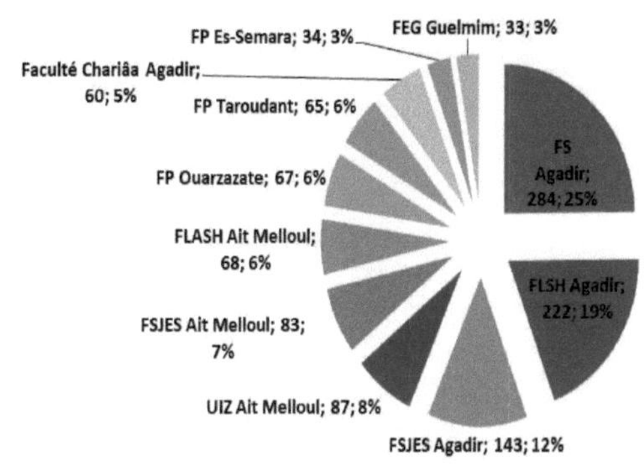

Accès Régulé: Répartition des enseignants par établissement (Tot;%)

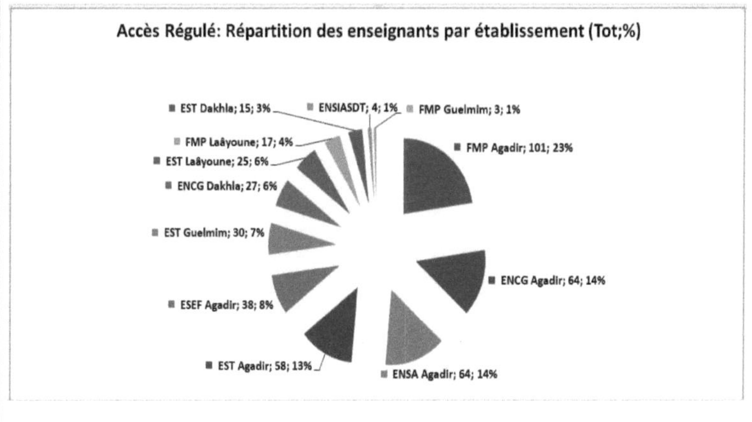

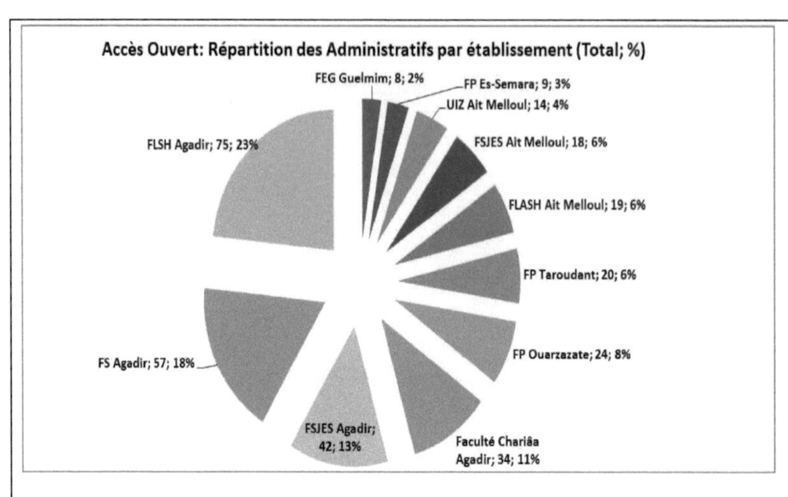

Accès Ouvert: Répartition des Administratifs par établissement (Total; %)
FEG Guelmim; 8; 2%
FP Es-Semara; 9; 3%
UIZ Ait Melloul; 14; 4%
FSJES Ait Melloul; 18; 6%
FLASH Ait Melloul; 19; 6%
FP Taroudant; 20; 6%
FP Ouarzazate; 24; 8%
Faculté Chariâa Agadir; 34; 11%
FSJES Agadir; 42; 13%
FS Agadir; 57; 18%
FLSH Agadir; 75; 23%

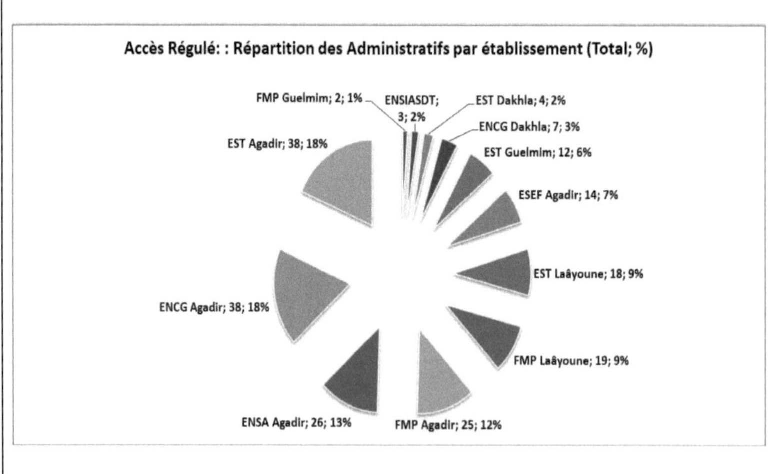

Accès Régulé: : Répartition des Administratifs par établissement (Total; %)
FMP Guelmim; 2; 1%
ENSIASDT; 3; 2%
EST Dakhla; 4; 2%
ENCG Dakhla; 7; 3%
EST Guelmim; 12; 6%
ESEF Agadir; 14; 7%
EST Laâyoune; 18; 9%
FMP Laâyoune; 19; 9%
FMP Agadir; 25; 12%
ENSA Agadir; 26; 13%
ENCG Agadir; 38; 18%
EST Agadir; 38; 18%

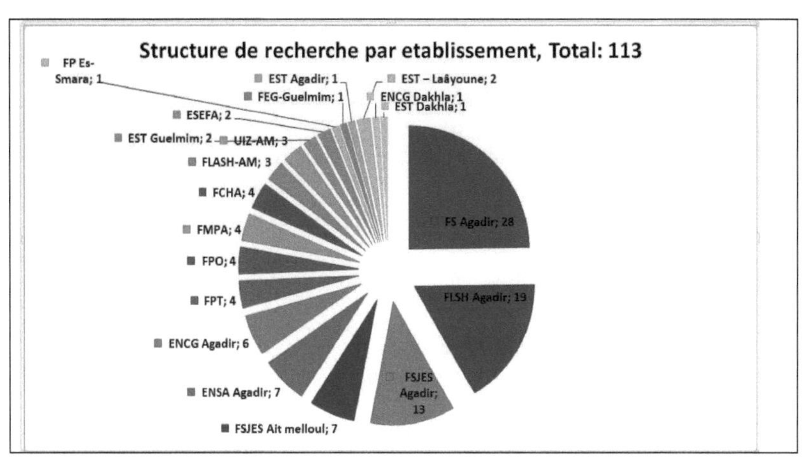

The following tables show in detail :

- Statistics on the various training courses by establishment and the number of students enrolled.
- Number of teachers and administrative staff per school
- Research structures
- Ibnou Zohr University budget revenues
- Current construction projects

	Establishment	Students in training (Tota)
Open access	Agadir Faculty of Legal, Economic and Social Sciences (FSJESA)	42074
	Faculty of Letters and Humanities Agadir (FLSH)	26817
	Faculty of Legal, Economic and Social Sciences Ait Melloul (FSJESAM)	25528
	Agadir Faculty of Science (FS)	9850
	Ait Melloul Faculty of Languages, Arts and Humanities (FLASH)	6766
	Faculty of Chariâa Agadir	6240
	Faculté Polydisciplinaire Es-Semara (FPS)	3951
	Ait Melloul Faculty of Applied Sciences (UIZ)	3568
	Taroudant Polytechnic Faculty (FPT)	3530
	Guelmim Faculty of Economics and Management	3359

	(FEGG)		
	Faculté Polydisciplinaire Ouarzazate (FPO)	3271	
Regulated access	Agadir National School of Business and Management (ENSA)	2833	
	École Supérieure de l'Education et de la Formation Agadir (ESEFA)	2449	
	National School of Applied Sciences Agadir (ENSA)	1522	
	Faculty of Medicine and Pharmacy Agadir (FMPA)	1516	
	Agadir School of Technology (ESTA)	1241	
	École Supérieure de Technologie Guelmim (ESTG)	973	
	Dakhla National School of Business and Management (ENCGD)	680	
	Laâyoune School of Technology (ESTL)	615	
	Laâyoune Faculty of Medicine and Pharmacy (FMPL)	519	
	Dakhla School of Technology (ESTD)	345	
	Guelmim Faculty of Medicine and Pharmacy (FMPG)	99	
	National School of Artificial Intelligence and Data Science (ENSIASDT)	60	

❖ Doctoral enrolment statistics by institution 2023-2024

Doctoral study centers (CED)	Establishments	New registrants	Total
Le Centre Des Études Doctorales en Sciences Et Techniques Et Sciences Médicales	ENSA Agadir	31	155
	FMP Agadir	13	
	FP Ouarzazate	6	
	FP Taroudant	10	
	FS Agadir	84	
	UIZ Ait Melloul	11	
Le Centre Des Études Doctorales En Sciences	Chariâa Ait Faculty Melloul	52	208
	FSJES Agadir	58	
	FSJES Ait melloul	65	

Juridiques Economiques Sociales & De Gestion	ENCG	33	
The Centre For Doctoral Studies In The Humanities, Arts And Educational Sciences	FLSH Agadir	63	86
	FLASH Ait Melloul	20	
	ESEF Agadir	3	
Total			**449**

❖ The ... teaching staff

For the current academic year, Ibnou Zohr University has 1,592 permanent lecturers and researchers, including 147 women, distributed across its various establishments as follows:

Establishme nts		Teachers (Total)
	FS Agadir	284
	FLSH Agadir	222
	FSJES Agadir	143
	UIZ Ait Melloul	87
	FSJES Ait Melloul	83
	FLASH Ait Melloul	68
Open access	FP Ouarzazate	67
	FP Taroudant	65
	Faculty of Chariâa Agadir	60
	FP Es-Semara	34
	FEG Guelmim	33
Total open access		1146
	FMP Agadir	101
	ENCG Agadir	64
	ENSA Agadir	64
	EST Agadir	58
	ESEF Agadir	38
	EST Guelmim	30

Regulated access	ENCG Dakhla	27
	EST Laâyoune	25
	FMP Laâyoune	17
	EST Dakhla	15
	ENSIASDT	4
	FMP Guelmim	3
Total regulated access		**446**
Total		**1592**

For the current academic year, the Ibnou Zohr University has 634 civil servants, including 249 women, distributed across the various establishments as follows:

Establishments		Administrative (Total)
Open access	FEG Guelmim	8
	FP Es-Semara	9
	UIZ Ait Melloul	14
	FSJES Ait Melloul	18
	FLASH Ait Melloul	19
	FP Taroudant	20
	FP Ouarzazate	24
	Faculty of Chariâa Agadir	34
	FSJES Agadir	42
	FS Agadir	57
	FLSH Agadir	75
Total open access		320
Regulated access	FMP Guelmim	2
	ENSIASDT	3
	EST Dakhla	4
	ENCG Dakhla	7
	EST Guelmim	12
	ESEF Agadir	14
	EST Laâyoune	18
	FMP Laâyoune	19
	FMP Agadir	25
	ENSA Agadir	26
	ENCG Agadir	38

	EST Agadir	38
Total regulated access		206
UIZ PRESIDENCY Agadir		108
Grand total		634

For the 2023-2024 academic year, Université Ibnou Zohr is offering its students courses covering almost every disciplinary field. Here is a list of the courses on offer, broken down by type of establishment.

ENCGA

Diploma	Branch titles
DENCG	Financial and Accounting Management
DENCG	Human Resources Management
DE-NCG	Audit and management control
DENCG	International Trade
DENCG	Marketing and Sales Action
DENCG	Advertising and Communication
MS	Sports management

ENCGD

Diploma	Branch titles
DENCG	Audit and Management Control
DENCG	Logistics Management
DENCG	International Trade
DENCG	Marketing and Sales Action
DENCG	Financial and Accounting Management
DENCG	Human Resources Management
MS	Economic Intelligence and Territorial Foresight

ENSIASD

Diploma	Branch titles
DI	Information Systems Management and Governance
DI	Software and Application Development

Diploma	Branch titles
DI	IT Security and Digital Trust
DI	Data Science, Big data & AI

ENSA

Diploma	Branch titles
2AP	Preparatory classes
DI	Industrial Engineering
DI	Electrical Engineering
DI	Finance and decision engineering
DI	Computer Engineering
DI	Energy and environmental engineering
DI	Mechanical Engineering
DI	Process, Energy and Environmental Engineering
DI	Building and civil engineering
MS	Embedded systems and industrial applications
MS	Energy efficiency and building control
MS	Financial engineering

ESTA

Diploma	Branch titles
DUT	BioIndustrial Engineering
DUT	Electronics, Electrical Engineering & Automated Systems
DUT	Computer Engineering
DUT	Marketing and Communication Techniques
DUT	Management Techniques
LP	Audit and Controlling (ACG)
LP	AUTOMATION AND BUILDING MANAGEMENT
LP	INTERNATIONAL TRADE AND LOGISTICS
LP	Water and Environmental Engineering

ESTD

Diploma	Branch titles
DUT	Food Process Engineering
DUT	ELECTRICAL ENGINEERING
DUT	Computer Engineering

Diploma	Branch titles
DUT	Management Techniques

ESTG

Diploma	Branch titles
DUT	Renewable energies and energy efficiency
DUT	Electrical Engineering
DUT	Computer Engineering
DUT	Mangement Techniques
LP	Renewable Energies and Processes
LP	Business intelligence and statistics
LP	Instrumentation and Systems
LP	Data science
LP	Computer and Network Security

ESTL

Diploma	Branch titles
DUT	Agro-Biological Engineering
DUT	Civil Engineering
DUT	Logistics for the Economy and Finance
DUT	Legal Techniques
DUT	Computer Engineering
LP	Renewable energies and seawater desalination
LP	Human Resources Management
LP	Media and communication techniques
LP	Legal and Financial Techniques
LP	Statistics and Business Intelligence
LP	Environmental engineering and development of local products
LP	Logistics and Quality Management
LP	Civil and Environmental Engineering

ESTO

Diploma	Branch titles
DUT	Network Management & Security
DUT	Data Engineering

ESEF

Diploma	Branch titles
LE	Bachelor of Education in Secondary Education - Mathematics
LE	Bachelor of Education in Secondary Education - Physical and Chemical Sciences
LE	Bachelor of Education in Secondary Education - Life and Earth Sciences
LE	Bachelor's degree in Education, specializing in primary education
LE	Bachelor of Education in Secondary Education - English Language
LE	Bachelor of Education in Secondary Education - French Language
M	Educational technologies and innovation

FCHARIAA

Diplôme	Intitulés des filières
L	الشريعة والقانون والمهن القضائية
L	الشريعة والقانون والمالية التشاركية
L	الشريعة والقانون والعلوم الشرعية
L	الشريعة والقانون والأسرة والرعاية الاجتماعية
L Excellence	الشريعة والاقتصاد التضامني
L Excellence	applied islamic sciences
L Excellence	الشريعة والدراسات القضائية المقارنة
M	قواعد الاجتهاد والتنزيل
M	التوثيق والعقار في الفقه المالكي والتشريع المغربي
M	التشريع والقضاء الأسري المغربي والمقارن

FEEG

Diploma	Branch titles
L	Economic Engineering
L	Financial Engineering
L	Accounting, Controlling and Auditing
L	Business and Marketing

L	Human Resources Management
L	Management of Social and Solidarity Economy Organizations
MS	Accounting, Controlling and Auditing
MS	Logistics and International Trade
M	Finance, Banking and Insurance

FLASH

Diplôme	Intitulés des filières
L	Linguistic, Literary, and Cultural Studies
L	Sciences du langage et de la communication
L	Lettres et Arts
L	البيئة وتدبير الأوساط الطبيعية
L	التهيئة والتنمية
L	Assistance sociale
L	الفنون والتراث
L	Anthropologie sociale
L Excellence	Information, communication
L Excellence	Digital Media and Translation
M	Transcultural and Memory studies
M	Lettres et Arts
M	التنمية والموارد الترابية

FLSH

Diplôme	Intitulés des filières
L	Littérature amazighe
L	Linguistique amazighe
L	English linguistics and literature
L	Littérature, Langue et Communication
L	Filología Hispánica
L	اللسانيات وديداكتيك اللغة العربية
L	الإبداع الأدبي والمهن الثقافية
L	الفقه والأصول
L	القرآن والحديث
L	التاريخ والحضارة
L	البيئة والتهيئة
L	مجتمع المعرفة والتحولات المعاصرة
M	Communication and Media in Cultural Studies
M	"Didactique du FLE: Culture et Médiation"

M	Tourisme, Communication et Développement	
M	Arts et Communication	
M	Applied Linguistics and English Language Teaching	
M	Comparative Studies In Literature	
M	اللغة والأدب بالجنوب المغربي	
M	علم النص وتحليل الخطاب	
M	تاريخ الجنوب المغربي: السلطة والمجتمع والدين	
M	الدراسات الصحراوية والأفريقية	
M	العلاقات الدينية والثقافية بين المغرب وأفريقيا جنوب الصحراء	
M	الخطاب الشرعي وتكامل العلوم	
M	InterculturalismoMarruecos y Mundo Hispanico	
M	Travail Social et développement	
M	Langue et culture amazighes	

FMPA

Diploma	Branch titles
DM	Doctor of Medicine
M	Medical Biotechnology

FMPL

Diploma	Branch titles
DM	Training for the Diplôme de Docteur en Médecine

FMPG

Diploma	Branch titles
DM	Training for the Diploma of Doctor of Medicine

FPO

Diploma	Branch titles
L	Film and audiovisual production management
L	Applied foreign languages and communication
L	Tourism, Culture and Sustainable Development
L	Audiovisual and Multimedia Techniques
L	Energy Engineering and Renewable Energies

L	Geosciences and Mineral Resource Development
L	Applied chemistry and valorization of natural substances
L	Mathematical Engineering
L	Cybersecurity
L	Econometrics
L	ACCOUNTING-FINANCE-TAX
L	Artificial Intelligence and Software Engineering
L	Design Thinking & UX / UI Design
Excellence	Film Art and Visual Aesthetics
M	Cinema, Audiovisual and Communication
M	Electronics-Advanced materials for new and renewable energies Renewables
M	Applied Mathematics for Data Science

FPS

Diplôme	Intitulés des filières
M	العقيدة الأشعرية بالغرب الإسلامي والامتداد الافريقي
L	الدراسات الشرعية المعاصرة
L	المهن القضائية
L	الوساطة والخدمة الاجتماعية
L	Langues, Communication et Traduction
M	الأسرة والرعاية الاجتماعية

Diploma	Branch titles
L	Biotechnology, Protection and Enhancement of Biological Resources
L	Biotechnologies and Health
L	Chemistry of materials and valorization of natural resources
L	Applied physical chemistry
L	Organic Chemistry and Sustainable Development
L	Applied geosciences
L	Geomatics Applied to Geosciences and the Environment
L	Software and IT Engineering
L	Software engineering

Diploma	Branch titles
L	Data science
L	Applied Mathematics
L	Mathematics and Applications
L	Electronics and Systems
L	Modern Physics
L	Energy and Renewable Energy
L	Materials science
L	Aquatic Systems and Aquaculture Production
Excellence	Software engineering
Excellence	Computer Engineering and Embedded Systems
Excellence	Data Analytics and Artificial Intelligence
M	BIODIVERSITY, BIOTECHNOLOGY AND SUSTAINABLE DEVELOPMENT
M	Fundamental Biology
M	Applied Organic Chemistry
M	Master in Advanced Multifunctional Materials and the Environment
M	Geosciences and Georesources
M	Data Science

Diploma	Branch titles
M	Mathematics applied to engineering sciences
M	Systems and Telecommunications S&T
M	Energy and Renewable Energies
MS	Distributed Computing Systems & BigData

UIZAM

Diploma	Branch titles
L	Data Analytics
L	Embedded Computing Systems
L	Mathematical engineering
L	Biology Applied to Plant Resources
L	Biotechnologies Applied to Animal Production
L	Applied Chemistry
L	Materials chemistry and water sciences
L	Thermal Engineering and Energy Efficiency
L	Industrial Technology Engineering
M	Embedded systems and digital services

Diplôme	Intitulés des filières
M	قانون الاعمال واليات تسوية المنازعات
M	العلوم الجنائية والأمنية
M	التدبير الاداري والمالي للجماعات الترابية
MS	Comptabilité, Contrôle De Gestion Et Audit
M	Analyse Et Politique Economiques
L	قانون الاعمال والمعاملات الرقمية
L	القانون الجنائي والعلوم الأمنية
L	المنازعات والمهن القانونية والقضائية
L	القانون المدني والعقاري
L	الرعاية الاجتماعية ومدونة الأسرة
L	الدراسات الإدارية والمالية
L	الدراسات الدستورية والسياسية
L	الدراسات الدولية
L	Comptabilité et Finance Appliquée
L	Comptabilité Controle de gestion Audit
L	Marketing et Management des organisations
L	Economie Appliquée
L	Econométrie
L Excellence	Comptabilité Contrôle Audit
L Excellence	Droit et Economie du Sport
L Excellence	Marketing, logistique et digital

Université Ibnou Zohr has 113 research facilities, accredited for the period 2022-2026, distributed as follows:

Domiciliary establishment	N.O.
FS Agadir	28
FLSH Agadir	19
FSJES Agadir	13
FSJES Ait melloul	7
ENSA Agadir	7
ENCG Agadir	6
FPT	4
FPO	4
FMPA	4
FCHA	4
FLASH-AM	3
UIZ-AM	3
EST Guelmim	2
ESEFA	2
FP Es-Smara	1
FEG-Guelmim	1
EST Agadir	1
EST - Laâyoune	2
ENCG Dakhla	1
EST Dakhla	1
Total	113

❖ Evolution of Scopus and WOS publications

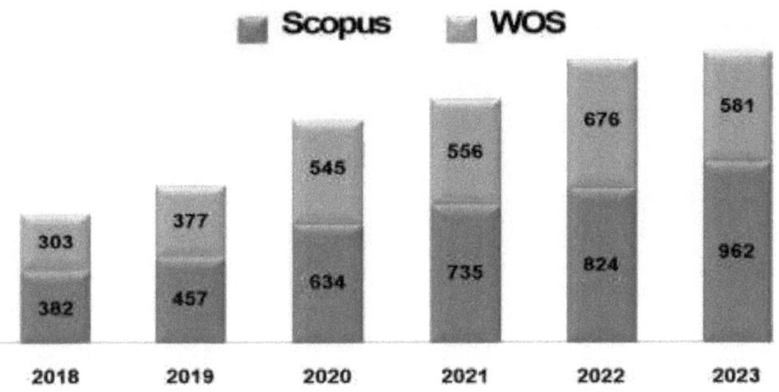

❖ Scientific events organized by establishments 2022-2023

Legal and economic sciences, Social and Management	Humanities, Arts and Sciences of Education	Science and Technology and Medical Sciences
202	98	58

❖ Participation in calls for projects

International: 33

National: 46

❖ Cooperation

As part of its international expansion, Ibnou Zohr University has established cooperative partnerships with numerous universities and research institutions around the world. A total of 151 agreements and conventions have been signed, including 104 national conventions and 47 international conventions. Among the national agreements, 62 partners are public, while the others are private.

❖ Mobility

Université Ibnou Zohr has registered a total of 458 international mobilities from 2020-2023.

421 Outgoing mobility

- 402 students ;

- 19 teachers.

37 Inbound mobility

- 18 students ;

- 16 teachers ;

- 3 administrative and technical staff.

❖ **Ibnou Zohr University budget revenues**

	2019	2020	2021	2022	2023	2024
State subsidy investment	106149200,00	72149200,00	123149200,00	189105080,00	160400400,00	147759400,00
State subsidy operation	100468650,00	96907400,00	103843400,00	123422000,00	140633769,00	151313000,00
Own revenues operation	9607155,88	6463026,60	9052114,04	7839556,49	8175392,02	
Own revenues investment	2480000,00	12000000,00	-	10000000,00	-	

❖ **Current construction projects**

1. Construction of a coding area at ibnou zohr university
2. Construction of a doctoral studies center and digital hub in Agadir
3. Construction of a scientific research block at the Faculty of Arts And human sciences in Agadir.
4. Construction of a technology hall at the National School of Science Applied to Agadir
5. Work on an extension to the ait melloul faculty of applied sciences (1st phase)
6. Work on an extension to the ait melloul faculty of applied sciences (2nd phase)
7. Construction work on the ait melloul education and training college (esef)
8. Construction of an extension to the ait melloul faculty

of languages, arts and humanities: (1st phase)

9. Construction of an extension to the ait melloul faculty
   of languages, arts and humanities: (2nd phase)
10. Project for the construction of a national graduate school of artificial intelligence and
    Data sciences in Taroudant
11. Construction of an extension to the Ouarzazate multidisciplinary faculty
12. Construction of an extension to the Es-smara multi-disciplinary faculty
13. Extension of the Dakhla School of Technology

IV. <u>Ibnou Zohr University strategies</u>

As an academic institution, the university plays a central role in the economic, social and cultural development of modern societies. To fulfill this mission, it must adopt robust development strategies and innovative approaches that respond to the changing needs of the contemporary world. This project explores the different development strategies and approaches that ibnou zohr university can adopt to remain relevant, competitive and effective.

> **Academic Development Strategy**

Academic development is at the heart of a university's mission. To stay at the cutting edge, a university must constantly review and update its academic programs in line with scientific advances, labor market needs and student expectations. Here are some key elements of an effective academic development strategy:

- **Program innovation**: Universities need to develop new programs that meet the emerging needs of industry and technology. For example, courses in artificial intelligence, sustainable development or cybersecurity can attract new students and meet current market demands.
- **Teaching Quality**: Improving the quality of teaching through in-service teacher training, the use of new pedagogical methods, and the integration of digital technologies is crucial to delivering quality education.

- **Research and Development (R&D)**: Universities need to invest in research, not only to produce new knowledge, but also to solve societal and economic problems. Collaborating with industry on applied research projects can also strengthen their role in economic development.

➢ **Institutional Development Strategy**

Institutional development is about how the university structures and organizes itself to achieve its goals. A robust institutional development strategy may include:

- **Governance**: Establishing effective governance with transparent and participative decision-making mechanisms is essential. This includes setting up boards of directors, involving stakeholders in governance, and establishing clear policies for resource management.
- **Infrastructure**: Investing in modern infrastructure, including green campuses, state-of-the-art laboratories and digital libraries, is vital to support academic and research activities.
- **Internationalization**: Developing partnerships with universities abroad, encouraging the international mobility of students and teachers, and offering bilingual or multilingual programs can enhance the university's global competitiveness.

➢ **Pedagogical and technological approaches**

Pedagogical and technological approaches are key to modernizing teaching and learning in universities. Here are some key approaches:

- **Student-centered learning**: This approach focuses on students' needs and interests, making them actors in their own learning. This can include methods such as project-based learning, collaborative learning and experiential learning.
- **Educational Technology**: Integrating technology into teaching, for example through online courses, interactive simulations and virtual reality tools, can enrich the learning experience and make it more accessible.
- **Continuing Education and Lifelong Learning**: Universities need to offer continuing education programs to enable professionals to update their skills. This approach responds to the growing need for requalification in an ever-changing job market.

A university cannot exist in a vacuum; it must actively engage with the community and assume social responsibility. This can mean :

- **Community partnerships**: Working with local organizations, businesses and public authorities to solve local problems, such as unemployment or social inequalities.
- **Public Service Programs**: Develop programs that encourage students to engage in public service activities, strengthening their sense of citizenship and their connection to the community.
- **Environmental responsibility**: Promote green initiatives on campus, such as recycling, the use of renewable energies, and raising awareness of the importance of environmental sustainability.

➢ Financing and Economic Sustainability

Funding is a crucial element in the implementation of development strategies. Universities need to explore various sources of funding to ensure their economic sustainability:

- **Diversification of revenue sources**: In addition to public funding, universities can seek private funding, develop fee-based continuing education activities, or create endowment funds.
- **Efficient Resource Management**: Ensure prudent and efficient management of financial and material resources to maximize their impact on the university's development.
- **Investing in Innovation**: Universities can invest in innovative initiatives, such as the creation of university start-ups or spin-offs, to generate additional income and encourage entrepreneurship.

The development strategies and approaches adopted by a university determine its long-term success. By integrating robust academic, institutional, pedagogical, community and financial strategies, universities can not only meet current needs, but also anticipate future challenges. A holistic and proactive approach is therefore essential to ensure that universities continue to play a central role in the development of modern societies.

V. <u>Development plan and approaches</u>

Law 01.00 stipulates that university establishments are created in the form of faculties, schools or institutes. They constitute the university's higher education and research structures. They group together departments corresponding to disciplines and fields of study and research, and services. They may also set up teaching, training, study and/or research centers, with the approval of the University Council.

✓ **Teaching autonomy :**

- Designing the training offer ;
- Proposal and adoption of training courses ;
- Creation of university diplomas.

✓ **Administrative and financial autonomy :**

- University presidents have been vested with financial, human resources and property management powers;
- University councils deliberate on all matters concerning the management of the university: creation of training courses and university structures, allocation of human and financial resources, university development strategy, etc.
- The possibility of acquiring stakes in innovative companies and creating subsidiary companies;
- The possibility of diversifying sources of funding (paid continuing education, paid services, creation of innovative business incubators, exploitation of patents and licenses, etc.);
- Creation of Public Interest Groups (GIP).

Drawing up a strategic development project has always been an important part of university life. It is first and foremost a phase of reflection based on a broadly participatory approach involving all the university's players, with the aim of improving mutual, human and institutional knowledge. Dialogue, consultation and respect for justice. All components contribute to the realization of this project. At the end of this process, which requires the approval of the University Council, the project becomes a contract. It commits those involved, researchers and administrators, for a 4-year period, to the objectives set, the resources envisaged and the evaluation of results.

The success of the Ibnou Zohr University development project depends not only on the support and commitment of the administrative team and all the University's components, but also on our ability to :

- Establishing a climate of trust and respect, the only way to ensure long-lasting, fruitful relationships with partners.
- Adopt a participative organization and use motivational techniques to promote commitment and improve team performance.
- Staying on course in terms of the objectives to be achieved, while encouraging synergies and collaborative work between the different sites in the design of projects.
- Manage decision-making regarding priorities when projects of equal importance are to be carried out.

The priority objective of the current Ibnou Zohr University development project is to offer high-quality initial and continuing training, with a better training-employment match, relevant, visible and high-level scientific research, a win-win partnership with the socio-economic sector, a rich and diversified academic life, and infrastructures that meet quality and safety standards in terms of equipment and layout.

To achieve this goal, we have adopted a development strategy based on three principles: Change with continuity (consolidation of milestones achieved), project-based management and a culture of excellence, belonging and solidarity.

To implement this strategy, we are adopting an approach based on the following guidelines:

- ✓ Implement a more aggressive policy towards companies, broadening our angle of attack as much as possible. All avenues of partnership should be explored, including continuing education, consulting, expertise, studies and applied research;
- ✓ Setting up a support process, from welcoming the student to helping with orientation or reorientation, all the way through to graduation;
- ✓ Encourage students to take responsibility for and participate in community life at the school (research clubs, film clubs, sports clubs, environmental clubs, IT clubs, etc.);
- ✓ Qualify the winner for professional integration or further studies;
- ✓ Offer professional qualifications to graduates for trades or jobs;
- ✓ Acquire skills and know-how in the trades ;

- ✓ Optimal use of human resources, their development, mobilization and involvement in the process of implementing the UIZ 2024-2028 development project;
- ✓ Implementation of the UIZ information system and introduction of the quality approach into the day-to-day running of the university. This means that all actions must be evaluated before and after the fact, so that services can be constantly improved;
- ✓ A better understanding of the economic and social environment, with a view to proposing appropriate training programs and conducting targeted research;
- ✓ Participatory approach within university structures ;
- ✓ Launch a creative process of international expansion. The UIZ must give itself the means to acquire a position as a major international institution;
- ✓ Developing and leveraging research potential through collaborations, doctoral training and research projects, because it is this potential that is the main yardstick of excellence;

Our project, while integrating the above-mentioned elements, takes into account the constraints inherent in any dynamic of change and falls within the realm of the reasonable and the feasible.

His ambition is to make Ibnou Zohr University :

- ❖ **A university ranked among the best Arab and African universities and in the top 1000 worldwide;**
- ❖ **A leading training center and advanced research facility;**
- ❖ **A tool for social and economic development at both regional and national levels;**
- ❖ **A university that is fully integrated into its region and open to the world.**

With this in mind, we plan to implement a series of actions designed to :
- Turn the university into a digital environment with a truly high-performance, integrated information system.
- Putting students' interests and society's needs at the heart of the university's concerns;
- Develop interdisciplinarity by enhancing inter- and intra-institution complementarity and synergy in the fields of training and R&D;
- Create new training courses better adapted to the socio-economic needs

of each region and the country;
- Adapt the current global training offer to the real needs of the job market and to the need for thinkers capable of ensuring the country's cultural and scientific development and influence;
- Encouraging international mobility of teachers and students;
- Structuring and developing continuing education ;
- Promoting pedagogical innovation ;
- Developing distance learning;
- Boost research structures and encourage openness to socio-economic operators;
- Encourage scientific production and patenting;
- To promote the faculty's scientific and cultural influence and its national and international openness;
- Improving the quality of welcome and the working environment in our facilities;
- Introduce new approaches to participative management, emphasizing consultation, openness, listening and flexibility;

VI. <u>Action plan</u>

As one of the region's leading academic institutions, Agadir's Ibnou Zohr University finds itself at a decisive turning point in asserting its role in the national and international educational landscape. As the world rapidly evolves with unprecedented challenges and opportunities, the university must adapt its strategies and objectives to meet the growing needs of its students, researchers and society in general.

For the period 2024-2028, Ibnou Zohr University is embarking on an ambitious strategic development plan aimed at strengthening its position as a leading institution. This plan is based on a clear vision and detailed strategic objectives to modernize its infrastructure, improve the quality of its teaching, foster innovation and internationalization, while consolidating its social responsibility and commitment to sustainable development.

The aim of this plan is to transform the university into a model of academic excellence, innovation and community involvement. Through concrete, measurable actions, Ibnou Zohr University aims to enhance the academic experience for its students, support cutting-edge research, and strengthen its ties with the local and international community.

To achieve these objectives, the Ibnou Zohr University development plan is structured around several key areas:

1. Improving the quality of teaching

- **1.1 Enhancing teachers' pedagogical skills :** Organize in-service training for teachers, focusing on innovative teaching methods, the use of educational technologies, and student-centered approaches.
- **1.2 Curriculum modernization:** Revise and update curricula to align them with job market requirements and scientific advances. Integrate cross-disciplinary skills such as critical thinking, project management and entrepreneurship.
- **1.3. Pedagogical infrastructure development:** Invest in infrastructure modernization (laboratories, digital libraries, connected classrooms) to foster an interactive, hands-on learning environment.

2. Strengthening Scientific Research and Innovation

- **2.1. Encourage Collaborative Research:** Promote research partnerships with national and international institutions, industries and research centers. Facilitate access to research funds to support innovative projects.
- **2.2 Creating Centers of Excellence:** Developing specialized research centers in key areas such as renewable energies, sustainable agriculture, ICT and social sciences.
- **2.3. Valorization of research and technology transfer:** Set up incubators and gas pedals to support the creation of start-ups based on the results of university research.

3. Governance and Management Development

- **3.1 Strengthening transparency and participation:** Involve stakeholders (teachers, students, administrative staff) in decision-making. Improve transparency in the management of financial and human resources.
- **3.2. Digitization of Administrative Services:** Implement digital solutions to optimize administrative management, improve the student experience and facilitate access to online services.
- **3.3. Strengthening leadership skills:** Train administrative managers and faculty leaders in the best practices of university management and leadership.

4. Internationalization and Partnerships

- **4.1. Development of international exchange programs:** Encourage student and teacher mobility through partnerships with foreign universities, exchange programs and international collaborations.
- **4.2. Attractiveness for international students:** Improve facilities for international students, offer programs in English, and promote the university on the international scene.
- **4.3. Cooperation with the private sector:** Strengthen links with local businesses and industries to promote students' professional integration and develop work-study programs.

5. Social responsibility and sustainable development

- **5.1 Integrating the Principles of Sustainable Development:** Incorporate sustainable development issues into academic programs, research and university management. Implement environmentally-friendly practices on campus (waste management, energy conservation, etc.).
- **5.2 Community Involvement:** Develop social initiatives and projects in collaboration with local communities to address social needs such as literacy, health and local economic development.
- **5.3. Promoting Equality and Inclusion:** Ensuring equal opportunities and promoting an inclusive environment for all students, whatever their origin, gender or economic situation.

6. Improving Student Services

- **6.1. Strengthen academic and psychological support:** Set up personalized support services for students, including psychological support, guidance and mentoring programs.
- **6.2. Improving student infrastructure :** Develop sports, cultural and recreational facilities on campus. Improve catering services and accommodation conditions.
- **6.3. Promoting student involvement:** Encourage student participation in university life through clubs, associations and volunteer projects.

Each axis is associated with specific objectives, detailed actions, and key performance indicators (KPIs) to measure progress. The commitment and collaboration of all members of the university community, as well as external partners, will be essential to the success of this plan.

This strategic plan marks the start of a new era for Ibnou Zohr University, with an ambitious vision of becoming a center of academic excellence and a key player in the development of the region and the country.

1. Improving the quality of teaching

1.1 Enhancing teachers' pedagogical skills

- **Objective:** Improve teaching practices and the adoption of new educational technologies.
- **Actions :**
  - **Organize quarterly teacher training workshops.**
    - **Sub-Target:** Train at least 80% of teachers in the use of educational technologies and innovative teaching methods by 2026.
    - **KPI:** Number of training courses organized, percentage of teachers trained.
    - **Schedule:** 2024-2026.
    - Department of Pedagogical Development, in collaboration with the faculties.
  - **Develop an online training platform dedicated to teachers.**
    - **Sub-goal:** Launch the platform by the end of 2025 and achieve a 70% participation rate among teachers by 2027.
    - **KPI:** Number of online courses available, course enrolment and completion rates.
    - **Schedule:** 2024-2025.
    - **Manager:** Digital Transformation Department.
  - **Set up a mentoring program for new teachers.**
    - **Sub-goal:** Ensure that each new professor has an experienced mentor during his or her first two years at the university.
    - **KPI:** Number of mentor/mentee pairs trained, mentee satisfaction rate.
    - **Timeline:** Start in 2024, annual follow-up.
    - **Responsible:** Academic Departments, under the coordination of the Human Resources Department.

For an even more detailed action plan for the Ibnou Zohr University of Agadir for the period 2024-2028, we will add sub-objectives, key performance indicators (KPIs), timelines, as well as designated leaders for each action.

1.2 Modernization of Academic Programs

- **Objective:** Adapt programs to changes in the job market and scientific advances.
- **Actions :**
  - **Create discipline-specific program review committees.**
    - **Sub-Goal:** Revise all academic programs by 2026.
    - **KPI:** Number of programs reviewed, employer and alumni satisfaction.
    - **Schedule:** 2024-2026.
    - **Lead:** Deans of faculties, in collaboration with experts from the private sector.
  - **Launch new interdisciplinary programs.**
    - **Sub-Goal:** Introduce at least five new interdisciplinary programs by 2028.
    - **KPI:** Number of programs launched, student enrolment rates.
    - **Schedule:** 2024-2028.
    - **Responsible:** Academic Council, with the approval of the University Council.
  - **Facilitate project-based learning in all curricula.**
    - **Sub-goal:** Integrate a practical project into 100% of courses by 2026.
    - **KPI:** Percentage of courses including a practical project, student satisfaction rate.
    - **Schedule:** 2024-2026.
    - **Responsible**: Program managers and teachers, under the supervision of the Academic Board.

1.3. Pedagogical infrastructure development

- **Objective:** Create a modern, interactive learning environment.
- **Actions :**
  - **Modernize classrooms with interactive equipment.**
    - **Sub-Target:** Equip 70% of classrooms with digital whiteboards and videoconferencing systems by 2026.
    - **KPI:** Number of rooms modernized, rate of technology use by teachers.
    - **Schedule:** 2024-2026.

- **Responsible**: Infrastructure and Logistics Department, in coordination with academic departments.
  o **Update scientific laboratories with state-of-the-art equipment.**
    - **Sub-goal:** Modernize 100% of laboratories by 2027.
    - **KPI:** Number of laboratories modernized, rate of equipment use by students and researchers.
    - **Schedule:** 2024-2027.
    - **Manager:** Scientific Research and Infrastructure Department.
  o **Create coworking and collaboration spaces.**
    - **Sub-goal:** Open at least three coworking spaces on campus by 2025.
    - **KPI:** Number of spaces created, occupancy rate and user satisfaction.
    - **Schedule:** 2024-2025.
    - **Manager:** Student Services and Infrastructure Department.

2. Strengthening Scientific Research and Innovation

2.1. Encouraging collaborative research

- **Objective:** Increase scientific output and national and international collaborations.
- **Actions :**
  o **Establish strategic partnerships with universities and research centers.**
    - **Sub-goal:** Sign at least ten new international partnerships by 2026.
    - **KPI:** Number of partnerships signed, number of publications co-authored.
    - **Schedule:** 2024-2026.
    - **Responsible:** Vice-President in charge of research, with the help of the deans of faculties.
  o **Organize international conferences and symposia.**
    - **Sub-goal:** Organize at least one international conference per specialty per year.

- **KPI:** Number of conferences organized, number of international participants.
      - **Timetable:** Annual, 2024-2028.
      - **Manager:** Research and Innovation Committee, in collaboration with the International Relations Office.
  - **Launch a collaborative research grant program.**
      - **Sub-Target:** Award at least 20 grants for collaborative research projects by 2027.
      - **KPI:** Number of grants awarded, impact of funded projects.
      - **Schedule:** 2024-2027.
      - **Responsible:** Office of Research and Innovation, in partnership with funding agencies.

2.2 Creating Poles of Excellence

- **Objective: To** become a leader in specific research fields.
- **Actions :**
  - **Develop specialized research centers.**
      - **Sub-goal:** Create at least five centers of excellence by 2028.
      - **KPI:** Number of centers created, number of publications and patents produced.
      - **Schedule:** 2024-2028.
      - **Coordinator:** Vice President, Research, with the support of the Deans.
  - **Secure funding to support clusters of excellence.**
      - **Sub-goal:** Raise at least 10 million dirhams for the clusters by 2026.
      - **KPI:** Amount of funds raised, number of projects financed.
      - **Schedule:** 2024-2026.
      - **Manager:** Corporate Relations and Partnerships Department.
  - **Create doctoral and post-doctoral programs.**
      - **Sub-goal:** Launch five new doctoral programs in centers of excellence by 2028.
      - **KPI:** Number of programs launched, PhD student enrolment rate.
      - **Schedule:** 2024-2028.

- **Lead:** Academic and Research Councils.

2.3. Promoting research and technology transfer

- **Objective:** Transform research results into concrete, useful innovations for society.
- **Actions :**
  - **Create a technology transfer office** to facilitate the protection of intellectual property rights and the commercialization of innovations resulting from research.
  - **Set up business incubators and gas pedals** to help researchers and students create innovative start-ups.
  - **Encourage researchers to take part** in innovation competitions and technology fairs to raise the profile of research results.
  - **Develop partnerships with industry** to test and apply technological innovations in industrial environments.

3. Governance and Management Development

3.1 Strengthening Transparency and Participation

- **Objective:** Improve university governance through transparency and stakeholder participation.
- **Actions :**
  - **Create advisory councils** made up of students, professors and administrative staff to participate in the university's strategic decisions.
  - **Implement transparent** budget and human resources **management systems**, with periodic reports accessible to all members of the university community.
  - **Organize annual discussion forums** on university management, to gather opinions and suggestions from all stakeholders.
  - **Regularly assess** student and staff **satisfaction** to adjust governance strategies accordingly.

3.2. Digitization of administrative services

- **Objective:** Optimize administrative management through digital solutions.
- **Actions :**
  - **Develop a single digital portal** for students, teachers and administrative staff, bringing together all services (registration, grade tracking, administrative requests).
  - **Automate** day-to-day **administrative processes** (registration, grade management, diploma issuance) to reduce lead times and improve efficiency.
  - **Train administrative staff** in digital tools and online management best practices.
  - **Implement a customer relationship management (CRM) platform** to improve interactions between the administration and students, as well as with external partners.

3.3. Strengthening leadership skills

- **Objective:** Develop leadership skills within university administration.
- **Actions :**
  - **Organize leadership training programs** for university executives, focusing on change management, strategic decision-making and team management.
  - **Establish a mentoring system** where experienced managers guide new managers in their duties.
  - **Promote managerial innovation** by encouraging pilot initiatives and experimental management projects within the university.
  - **Regularly assess the performance of** administrative **managers** to identify training needs and adjust professional development strategies.

4. Internationalization and Partnerships

4.1. Development of International Exchange Programs

- **Objective:** Strengthen the university's international outlook through student and teacher mobility.
- **Actions :**

- Establish exchange agreements with partner universities abroad, enabling students to spend a semester or academic year at another institution.
- Promote international exchange programs by informing students and facilitating administrative procedures for mobility.
- Encourage teachers to take part in mobility programs for teaching or research assignments at partner institutions abroad.
- Organize international events (conferences, workshops, cultural festivals) to promote intercultural exchange and international cooperation.

4.2. Attracting international students

- **Objective:** Attract more international students and diversify the student body.
- **Actions :**
  - **Improve facilities for** international students, including support services, adapted housing and integration programs.
  - **Offer teaching programs in English** and other languages to attract students from around the world.
  - **Promote the university internationally** by participating in student fairs, collaborating with recruitment agencies, and using digital marketing strategies.
  - **Set up a dedicated service for international students** to help them with administrative, academic and personal matters.

4.3. Cooperation with the private sector

- **Objective:** Strengthen links with companies to promote professional integration and innovation.
- **Actions :**
  - **Develop partnerships with local and international companies** to create work-study programs and professional internships.
  - **Organize job forums and company-university days** to facilitate dialogue between students and potential employers.
  - **Create corporate chairs** within the university to foster innovation in specific fields (e.g. emerging technologies, sustainable development).

- o **Include private-sector professionals** on academic program review committees to ensure they are in line with market needs.

5. Social responsibility and sustainable development

5.1 *Integrating the Principles of Sustainable Development*

- **Objective:** to make the university a model of environmental and social sustainability.
- **Actions :**
  - o **Incorporate sustainability issues** into all academic programs, including compulsory courses and sustainability projects.
  - o **Implement green practices** on campus, such as waste management, reducing water and energy consumption, and promoting renewable energies.
  - o **Create a sustainability committee** to monitor environmental initiatives and propose new actions to reduce the university's carbon footprint.
  - o **Encourage research projects** on sustainable development and ecological innovations, by offering specific grants and facilitating partnerships with NGOs and green businesses.

5.2 *Community involvement*

- **Objective:** Strengthen the university's social impact in the Agadir region and beyond.
- **Actions :**
  - o **Develop community service programs** where students and staff can contribute to local projects (e.g. literacy programs, support for local start-ups).
  - o **Organize workshops and seminars** for local community members on topics such as education, health and economic development.
  - o **Establish partnerships with NGOs and public institutions** to support social and environmental initiatives in the region.
  - o **Promote** student **civic engagement** through volunteer programs and extracurricular activities focused on community development.

5.3. Promoting equality and inclusion

- **Objective: To** ensure an inclusive and equitable environment for all members of the university community.
- **Actions :**
    - **Implement policies of non-discrimination** and support for students from disadvantaged backgrounds, as well as those with disabilities.
    - **Develop scholarship programs** for deserving students from low-income families.
    - **Promote the inclusion of cultural diversity** by organizing intercultural events, workshops on tolerance, and fostering open dialogue between different groups.
    - **Create an Office of Inclusion and Equal Opportunity** to monitor and promote initiatives to strengthen equality on campus.

6. Improving Student Services

6.1. Strengthening academic and psychological support

- **Objective: To** support students throughout their academic and personal careers.
- **Actions :**
    - **Create academic counseling centers** to offer personalized assistance to students in course selection, career planning and academic stress management.
    - **Set up a psychological support service** accessible to students to help them overcome personal and emotional challenges.
    - **Develop student mentoring programs** where more advanced students or alumni accompany new students to facilitate their integration and academic success.
    - **Offer personal development workshops** on topics such as time management, revision techniques, and academic-life balance.

6.2. Improving student infrastructure

- **Objective:** To offer modern infrastructures adapted to students' needs.

- **Actions :**
    - ○ **Modernize university residences** to offer comfortable, adapted living conditions, including study, leisure and social areas.
    - ○ **Develop sports and cultural facilities** on campus to encourage a healthy, balanced lifestyle among students.
    - ○ **Improve university catering services** by offering a variety of healthy, affordable options adapted to different diets.
    - ○ **Create spaces for relaxation and socializing** on campus, such as student cafés, gardens and coworking spaces.

6.3. Promoting student commitment

- **Objective:** Encourage students to get involved in university life and develop their skills outside the classroom.
- **Actions :**
    - ○ **Support student clubs and associations** by offering them space, funding and advice to organize a variety of activities (cultural, sporting, academic).
    - ○ **Organize competitions and challenges** (hackathons, start-up competitions, academic debates) to stimulate students' creativity and innovative spirit.
    - ○ **Encourage student involvement in volunteer projects** and community initiatives, in partnership with local and national organizations.
    - ○ **Create a student innovation fund** to finance innovative projects proposed by students, with support for the development and realization of ideas.

The Ibnou Zohr University of Agadir's 2024-2028 Action Plan is an ambitious roadmap to take the institution to new heights of academic excellence and social responsibility. Through targeted strategic initiatives and measurable objectives, the plan aims to strengthen the university's position as a hub of knowledge, innovation and community engagement.

With a focus on academic quality, research innovation and internationalization, the university is committed to offering first-rate training and supporting cutting-edge research projects that respond to global challenges. At the same time, governance and management will be optimized to ensure efficient and transparent administration, while sustained efforts will be made to improve student services and infrastructure.

The integration of the principles of sustainable development and social responsibility is at the heart of this plan, illustrating the university's commitment to contributing positively to the community and preserving the environment. Planned sustainability and community engagement initiatives will aim to promote a positive impact and strengthen links between the university and its regional environment.

The success of this plan will depend on close collaboration between all stakeholders, including academic and administrative staff, students, external partners and the local community. Continuous evaluation of progress and flexibility to adjust strategies in line with developments and needs will be crucial to achieving the objectives set.

In conclusion, Ibnou Zohr University's 2024-2028 Action Plan is a strong statement of its ambition to transform itself into a nationally and internationally recognized institution of excellence. It reflects a clear commitment to innovation, quality and social impact, while preparing the university to meet future challenges with resilience and determination. The success of this strategy will be the fruit of a collective effort, a shared vision, and a determination to build a bright academic and social future for all members of the university community.

VII. <u>CONCLUSION</u>

It is in the context of major changes in the structure and mission of Moroccan universities, in the face of challenges linked to changes brought about by globalization and new technologies, that we propose this development project for the Agadir Faculty of Science. It has been designed to be consistent with the Faculty's missions, resources and evolution, and within the framework of Ibn Zohr University's general policy.

This opening project expresses :

> - One ambition: development;
> - One policy: university reform and the emergency plan;
> - The objectives to be achieved, while specifying the resources to be deployed for success.

The Faculty's overall development project, whose general objectives set out the prospects for development and improvement, as well as the indicators for monitoring them, will only be successful if everyone - teachers, administrative and technical staff, and students - fully plays the role assigned to them, and actively participates in defining and achieving common objectives.

These objectives can be summarized as follows:

- ✓ the quality of student intake and integration;
- ✓ Implement, obtain the support of all stakeholders for the university process, find the necessary funding to carry it out;
- ✓ To offer our students innovative, highly employable training courses, supported by top-quality supervision;
- ✓ Listening, analyzing, motivating, raising awareness, providing food for thought, stimulating or supporting action, dialoguing, initiating innovative actions, consulting before making decisions, and always communicating to explain choices, make them understood and applied;
- ✓ Ensuring good working conditions for teachers and administrative staff:

- ✓ Consistently transparent management. Management based on delegated decision-making, evaluation, ex-post control and accountability;

- ✓ Be more open to the socio-economic environment;

- ✓ Encourage people to develop projects for the company by giving them the means to do so, within a clearly defined framework;

- ✓ Establish academic, scientific, cultural and sporting partnerships;

To achieve this, the success of this project will require the awareness, mobilization, enhancement and motivation of all of the establishment's bodies, which will in turn generate comments, questions and suggestions that will enable corrections to be made, and can only enrich it and generate a collective commitment and buy-in from all players in order to succeed in this challenge.

The annual assessment will be used to make certain adjustments to the actions set out in the action plan, to ensure that it is carried out in an evolutionary manner, and to propose corrective actions to maintain the course set.

The project will be regularly monitored through the production of annual reports, which will be presented to the school board.

It will therefore be a "strong" joint project that the establishment will strive to implement throughout its term of office, adapting it to any new needs that may arise and resolutely adopting a multidisciplinary approach.

VIII. <u>References</u>

1- The Plan to Accelerate the Transformation of the Esri Ecosystem (Pacte Esri-2030)

2- The National Education and Training Charter

3- Bill 01-00

4- Law 51-17

5- Legislative and regulatory provisions

6- Action Plan 2017-2022 of the Ministry of National Education, Vocational Training, Higher Education and Scientific Research The Strategic Vision of Reform 2015-2030

7- University Statistics, Evaluation and Prospecting Department

8- Data from Ibn Zohr University

9- Website of the Ministry of Higher Education, Scientific Research and Innovation

10- Saaid Amzazi, Mohamed V University development project

11- Omar Halli, Ibn Zohr University development project

12- Abdelaziz Bendou, ENCG Agadir development project, 2011-2015

13- Idriss Mansouri, Hassan II University development project, 2013-2017

14- Projet d'établissement 2007-2010 Université JEAN MONNET SAINT ETIENNE

15- Mattieu Gallou, Université de Bret Occidentale development project

16- Séminaire " L'aide au pilotage des établissements : démarches et outils " March 27, 2002. Agence de modernisation des universités et établissements. Services Department 103, boulevard Saint-Michel 75005 Paris

17- Development Plan for the Souss Massa Region 2022-2027

18- Statistics from the Ministry of Industry, Investment, Commerce and the Digital Economy

19- Ibn Zohr University website and its components

20- CRI Souss Massa website

21- CRI Daraa Tafilalt website

22- Haut-commissariat au plan: www.hcp.ma

23- http://www.rdh50.ma/fr/index.asp

24- Learning in presence and at a distance. Une définition des dispositifs hybrides by Bernadette CHARLIER, Nathalie DESCHRYVER and Daniel PERAYA | Lavoisier | Distances et savoirs 2006/4 - Volume 4 ISSN 1765-0887 | pages 469 à 496

Printed by Books on Demand GmbH, Norderstedt / Germany